CREATING A HOME

FINISHING TOUCHES

WARD LOCK

CONTENTS

A WARD LOCK BOOK
First published in the UK in 1997
by Ward Lock, Wellington House, 125 Strand,
London WC2R 0BB
A Cassell imprint
Copyright © Eaglemoss Publications Ltd 1997
Based on *Creating a Home*
Copyright © cover design Ward Lock 1997
All rights reserved
Distributed in Australia by New Holland Publishers Pty Ltd,
3/2 Aquatic Drive, Frenchs Forest, NSW, Australia 2086
Distributed in Canada by Cavendish Books Inc., Unit 5, 801
West 1st Street, North Vancouver, B.C. Canada V7P 1PH
A British Library Cataloguing in Publication Data block for
this book may be obtained from the British Library
ISBN 0 7063 7650 1
Printed in Spain by Cayfosa Industria Grafica
10 9 8 7 6 5 4 3 2

INTRODUCTION

This delightful book is devoted to the fun part of furnishing and decorating a home – adding the finishing touches which stamp your personality and taste on every room. Colour photographs provide a rich library of ideas, and the text explains the design principles behind them.

Finishing Touches is also very practical. The opening chapters on pictures and mirrors show how to find the best height to hang them, how to work out pleasing groups of differently sized pictures and how to place mirrors to make rooms look bigger.

Almost any decorative items can be built up into an artistic and interesting collection. You will find chapters on displaying china, treasured objects of all sorts, glassware and dried flowers. The art of arranging things attractively is extended in a practical way with sections on siting houseplants and creating table settings.

Finishing Touches is packed with soft furnishing ideas: co-ordinating tablecloths; decorative bedheads, both simple and ornate; unusual ways of using patchwork and making cushions; dressing up bay windows and using sheer curtains.

An important part of the book covers adding original finishing touches when redecorating. For example, how to use broken colour paint finishes or stencilled patterns on walls, embellish them with wallpaper borders or pick out architectural details such as mouldings and panelling in contrasting colours. Further sections show ideas for painting old furniture to match or contrast with room schemes; adding dado rails to recapture a period flavour; and creative ways of using timber cladding and ceramic wall tiles.

Whether your interest lies in sewing, painting, picture framing, do-it-yourself or building up a collection of anything from fine porcelain to old keys, this book will help you to apply your talents to best advantage.

Hanging Pictures

Most rooms look more welcoming if they contain pictures. These needn't be expensive originals; reproduction prints and posters can be every bit as attractive and effective. But, whether a valuable family heirloom or a 'cheap and cheerful' poster, a picture must be hung where it can be easily seen and enjoyed.

The mistake most often made is to hang pictures too high. As well as being impossible to see without craning your neck, pictures hung too high can make the viewer feel a bit like a dwarf.

Relationships Not only should a picture be hung at the right level, it should also relate to other objects in the room. A picture hung on an otherwise empty wall often seems lost and unconnected, as if it arrived there by accident.

Instead, place a picture above a table, sofa, desk, sideboard, bookcase or fireplace – in fact, any piece of furniture or architectural detail that will visually 'anchor' it. This is particularly true of small pictures. Large paintings or posters can command a blank wall, but again, few people have pictures big enough to stand on their own.

Positioning You can hang a picture centrally above a piece of furniture, or to one side – whatever looks best. But remember, if all the pictures in a room are hung in the same way – each centred above a piece of furniture, for instance – the effect can be boring. Try hanging one or two off-centre.

Part of a group

This picture is hung quite low and arranged as part of the group of lamp, bowl and vases. For this sort of off-centre arrangement the picture usually looks best hung above a spot about one third along the length of the table below.

▽ *Kitchen lines*
The frame of this picture aligns with the cupboard top and the tile border.

BRIGHT IDEA

THE RIGHT HEIGHT
The centre of a picture should be no higher than eye level – halfway between standing and seating eye level is the best solution.

△ *Pairing up*
A pair of matched pictures hung symmetrically over a sofa creates a formal look. Note how the space between the two is the same as the space between the bottom of the pictures and the top of the sofa.

◁ *Connections*
Hanging a large picture fairly low over a plain sofa makes good design sense. This is a painting but some modern fabrics lend themselves to being stretched over a batten framework to make a large, inexpensive but effective picture.

Grouping Pictures

When it comes to grouping pictures, before banging holes in the wall, think about how they relate to one another. **The theme** In effect, the group works as a single unit, so ideally the pictures should have something in common. The most obvious example of this is a set of prints; these should all be the same size and have a common theme. A random group of prints can be given harmony by mounting and framing them to match.

Your pictures might have similar colouring – black and white prints for instance – or be all photographs. In this case no further link is necessary.

If the group have a strong subject theme – cats or children perhaps – a variety of media, shapes and frames can be mixed together very successfully.

Even if you can find no link do not despair, arranging your choice within a fairly controlled framework can hold the group together.

Arrangements Measure the amount of wall you have available, then mark out this area on the floor with string or newspaper. Experiment with various groupings to find the most pleasing one. When you are satisfied, very lightly indicate the area of your 'frame' on the wall. Then mark the position of the first picture, usually the largest one, and hang this, follow with the next most important placing and so on (see Bright Idea, overleaf). Check the spacing as you go.

▽ *Artful arrangement*
The charm of this arrangement of flower paintings is in its deceptively casual appearance. The large picture was hung; those either side centred on it; then the last placed with its top centred on the one next to it.

BRIGHT IDEA

Work out arrangement on the floor, marking out the basic guide lines with string or on sheets of newspaper.

Below are a selection of groupings which can be adapted to suit your particular needs.

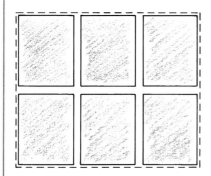

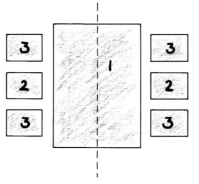

1 Pictures of the same size work best in a square or rectangle. The arrangement depends for its success on the pictures lining up absolutely accurately and all vertical spaces being equal.

2 One large picture and a set of six small ones can be arranged symmetrically. Position the large picture, then a small one centrally on each side. Place the other pictures, equally spaced on either side of them.

3 Rectangular and square pictures of varying sizes can be arranged in two rows. The top row 'hangs' from one horizontal line, the bottom row 'stands' on another. The sides should also be aligned.

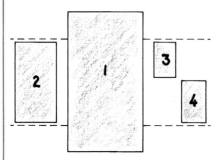

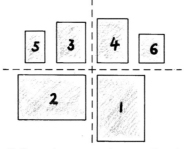

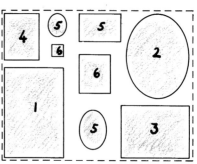

4 Pictures of varying sizes can be grouped with the largest in the middle; the next centrally on one side; then the third and fourth to line with the top and bottom of the second.

5 Group pictures around a cross. Place the largest pictures below the horizontal line balancing them with smaller ones above. Work in sequence as indicated.

6 Position a mixture of shapes within a formal framework. Starting with the largest pictures, fill in the corners; add any which touch the outside edge; then fill in the spaces with the rest.

◁ **Modern simplicity**
A selection of posters in similar colourings and with matching frames rest on the same invisible horizontal line; they are equally spaced and centrally placed on the wall. The geometric feel of the arrangement suits the plainness of the room and the horizontal line makes it seem wider.

▷ **In nostalgic mood**
These objects and old photographs grouped over a wash stand have been chosen to complement this turn-of-the century interior. The basis of the design is a horizontal line from which pictures and signs hang. A large oval sepia photograph is placed over the main group and a basket of dried flowers is set below it and off-centre. The latter is balanced by a plant on the wash stand below.

▽ **Quiet prints**
In this arrangement a group of prints on a variety of subjects almost fill one wall of a modern dining room. All have white backgrounds and simple chrome frames. Three of the pictures 'hang' from one horizontal line; the others 'stand' on another. The colours echo those used in the room.

△ Mixed media

When you have a lot of pictures in different styles and media to hang, working within a fairly formal framework gives them unity. Here a variety of prints, sketches and watercolours of people more or less fill a wall. The basis of the arrangement is the bottom line, with the side lines established slightly less strongly. The top is a 'skyline' which gives interest to the design.

▷ Perfect prints

A set of six prints is the most straightforward of all groups to arrange. The classic arrangement is a formal rectangular one made up of two rows of three. They should all be framed and mounted in the same way and be evenly spaced. In this case black-and-white subjects have been mounted and framed in a colour to pick up the dominant one in the room – coral red.

Memories on Display

Simple but sophisticated 'can't fail' cameras and cheaper processing have made photography more popular than ever before. Even though most people own a large collection of family and holiday photographs, pictures still tend to be hidden in albums or consigned to drawers, rather than being put on display where memories can be enjoyed and shared.

A display of photographs adds warmth and interest to any room — as well as providing a happy reminder of well-loved faces and places. Pictures can simply be mounted in a collection of frames and displayed on a small table.

Look for frames in a variety of sizes, so that the tallest ones can be positioned at the back, giving a balanced display. You can find frames in junk shops, or you can buy a variety of traditional and modern frames at department stores and picture framers. These can be ready-made, or designed for self-assembly to fit a particular photograph.

If you have several small face-only pictures to display it is worth buying a 'picture tree'. This is a small stand fitted with hooks for hanging miniature circular frames. Another alternative is a clear plastic box which displays a different picture on each face.

A wall-mounted display of framed photographs looks especially effective if the pictures are a variety of shapes and sizes. Choose a theme for your display for extra impact. You could, for instance, have a collection showing members of the family from babyhood onwards, family pets or holiday scenes.

Photographs should be well lit so that they can be seen at their best and enjoyed to the full. A wall display can be illuminated from above by a picture light. Avoid beaming light on to the pictures from the front as it will reflect in the glass and makes them difficult to see. Photographs on a table are best lit by a table lamp which will shine a pool of light down on to them.

Gallery style
Photographs decorating an ultra-modern bedroom are displayed in a suitably modern style, framed and mounted as if in a gallery of modern pictures. They rest on timber edges so can be moved and added to at will.

MAKE A MINI GALLERY
Display a collection of wedding photographs in one large frame. Use mounting cards with squares, ovals and circles cut in it to mask unwanted parts and create a harmonious arrangement of shapes.

△ **Fancy frames**
This small display of family portraits grouped on a side table is co-ordinated and enhanced by the use of very attractive art nouveau-style frames. The matching art nouveau lamp not only completes the arrangement stylistically, but also casts a soft overhead light on the photographs.

▷ **Historical interest**
A happy jumble of old photographs in sepia and black and white fills what might have been a dull corner with human interest. Although they are deliberately grouped haphazardly the landscape-format picture hung at the top knits the collection together into an artistic whole.

Living Room Wall Displays

A group of objects arranged on a wall makes an interesting alternative focal point to pictures. Such an arrangement usually works best with a theme to hold it together and a collection, by its very nature, fulfills this requirement.

Textiles, fans, plates and plaques, masks, hats and menus lend themselves to this treatment, as do bygones such as old tools and kitchen equipment.

Three-dimensional objects in a variety of shapes and sizes do not always call for a formal geometric arrangement. The subject often dictates how you approach the grouping. Decoy ducks, all of similar size and shape, work well in formal rows. Memorabilia, on the other hand, because of its personal nature, calls for a more relaxed treatment.

An arrangement, however informal, should not be allowed to straggle in a meaningless way; it should be closely grouped for a harmonious unity. For maximum impact it also needs to be balanced by surrounding space.

If you have a very large collection, think about displaying just a part of it. When things are on the wall for a long time they tend to become over-familiar and you find you no longer notice them. If this happens, you can replace them with more from your store.

Collecting often becomes addictive. You can allow for the resultant expansion in your grouping, perhaps creating an arrangement at one end of a wall — by a door or in a corner over a table. As the collection grows you can extend the display.

Pipes and pot lids
Small items often work best mounted together. Here sets of light coloured pot lids and clay pipes are mounted on dark hessian, dark keys on light. All have matching light pine recessed frames.

△ Wading birds

Water fowl are wittily arranged in a diamond pattern which overlays the grid on the wallcovering of this living room. The rod on which each is perched is attached to a simple metal bracket. Flat-bottomed decoy ducks could be arranged in the same pattern, but on small wooden bracket shelves.

▽ Within a rectangle

A set of fairly disparate objects is given unity by arranging them within a rectangle. Natural colours and materials – greeny shades, wood and brass – provide a further link. The central heating thermostat has been cleverly incorporated into the grouping in the top left corner.

▷ Over the stairs

The blank wall over a stairwell has been completely filled with a selection of tools and farm implements. The side walls frame the arrangement.

Mirror Images

Mirrors are more than simply decorative. They can be used deceptively to play with light and space.

If positioned opposite or adjacent to windows, mirrors bring extra light to rooms and are particularly useful in small dark areas. Large areas of mirror can create an illusion of greater space; an entire wall of mirror may double the width or length of a room, while a mirrored recess on either side of a fireplace gives the appearance of a long room with a central fireplace.

Where skirting may interrupt the illusion that a full-length mirror would create, a channel can be installed at floor level behind the carpet to carry the mirror. Alternatively, place some-thing in front of the mirror to disguise the skirting: a plant trough, sofa or side table add interest and also protect people from walking into the glass.

Always make sure that a mirror reflects something of interest – a picture, plant group or view of a garden. Thought should also be given to a mirror's doubling effect. A quarter-circle headboard looks like a semi-circular one when placed adjacent to a mirror. And remember if using a chequerboard tiling pattern by a mirror the effect will be lost unless half tiles are put next to the mirrored wall.

The combination of mirrors and glass can be exciting and works especially well in alcoves where, if ornaments are placed on glass shelves with a mirror behind them, they seem to float. But make sure that both sides of the objects are visually attractive.

△ *Double accent*
In this cloakroom the mirror plays a decorative as well as practical role. Diagonal lines help to make a room appear wider; in this case the effect of the tiling is accentuated by hanging a mirror in a diagonal position. In such a tiny space a simple colour scheme works best. Here furniture and accessories are picked out in a crisp blue and white.

◁ *Illusion of space*
A large mirror creates a focal point and gives an illusion of greater space in this small bedroom. Different standpoints reflect different parts of the room and a view of the garden through the window. Notice how a simple bunch of flowers placed against a mirror becomes a sizeable display.

▷ Two-way image

At first glance this bathroom appears to lead into a similar room through an opening. In fact, the effect is brought about by running a plainly-edged mirror behind the twin basins. Note the clever positioning of the second poster reflected in the mirror which adds to the illusion.

▽ *Reflected interest*

An ornamental mirror over a table reflects dressers on the other side of a large living room/kitchen and another room through the doorway between them. By adding interest to a plain wall and bringing light to the dark end of the room it could almost be a window.

Arranging Glass

The most characteristic aspect of glass is that light passes through it, so make the most of this fact when creating a display.

A selection of vases, with or without flowers, enlivens a windowsill as it catches the light.

Glass on glass gives an almost unreal sense of fragile objects floating on air; even the most mundane things take on a special aura.

Glass- or mirror-topped tables are perfect for this type of display. Choose all one type of object for maximum impact – a collection of drinking glasses, some glass animals or a group of bottles for example.

To make the most of glass at night, you will need to light it well. Lighting from above or below is the best choice. This could take the form of a downlighter mounted in the ceiling or incorporated into a built-in display unit.

As glass is transparent, a little light goes a long way. Providing the shelves as well as the displayed objects are glass, a single light is sufficient.

A ceiling-mounted downlighter can be focused to bring a table display to life. Alternatively, an inexpensive, free-standing uplighter is an effective way to light a glass-topped side table but make sure it is positioned so as not to dazzle the occupants of the room.

Finally, remember that glass shows every speck of dirt and must be kept sparkling clean to remain looking good.

▽ *Mirror image*
This arrangement, lit by daylight filtered through a venetian blind, takes advantage of the fact that the curves of the objects distort shapes seen through them. The slats of the blind seem to be bent in a variety of ways. The display gains impact from the mirrored surface.

△ *Alcove arrangement*
A selection of glass arranged on glass shelves is lit from above by a fitting mounted into a bathroom alcove. The top two shelves are filled with clear white and bluish glass bottles, which let light through. Colour and a change of shape are kept for the solid bottom shelf – deep blue vases and goblets.

△ On the sill

A variety of vases are given a sense of unity by being grouped together in front of a curtainless window. Flowers in some of the vases help to soften the plainness of the window and to give a degree of privacy. A balance is kept between tall and low arrangements and plant colours are kept to simple yellow, green and white.

◁ Glowing simplicity

The stylish simplicity of an arrangement of classical shapes on a marble-topped antique chest complements the modern painting above. A group of large, rounded white shapes are counterbalanced by the small, slim, dark lustre vase. As the white jars are opaque it is possible to hide a very small lamp behind them. This gives the two nearest to the light source a lovely pearly glow. Night lights would give a similar effect but must be placed so as not to be a fire hazard or damage the wall or the glass.

Decorating with Rugs

The spectrum of rugs available ranges from oriental and traditional patterns to zingy modern designs; they do not have to be expensive to be attractive.

The choice Kelims, flat-weave Turkish rugs in geometric designs and rich earth colours, are the least expensive oriental rugs and work well with country house chintzes or with modern stripes and checks. Most often they are made of wool and are extremely hard-wearing and with age the colours actually tend to soften and improve.

There are also very acceptable copies of the more expensive oriental carpets which create the same effect as the real thing. It is well worth looking out for secondhand oriental carpets; these can often be picked up quite cheaply through advertisements in the newspaper or by attending auctions and sales of household effects.

Dhurries, usually in muted pastel colours on a creamy background, are available in wool or cotton and span a range of sizes and prices. Many dhurries, particularly the large wool ones, are fairly formal and work well in a modern, sophisticated pastel coloured room scheme.

At the cheapest end of the market there are all sorts of flat-woven cotton rugs available from chain stores, in a variety of designs and colourways. They are an ideal way to give a room a lift without a big financial commitment.

Colour schemes Rugs have a variety of roles to play in decorating a room. A monochromatic design, for instance, can be given a focus with just one dramatic rug.

One of the devices an interior designer uses to pull the various components of a room scheme together is to choose a rug to echo certain colours and design elements of the fabrics, wallcoverings and furniture. Conversely, you can use a rug as your inspiration and select furnishings to echo its colours and pattern.

On the floor Rugs can be used to 'hold' a seating area together or to split up a multi-activity room. In a long or L-shaped living/dining room, for instance, two matching or sympathizing rugs can be used – one to anchor the seating area and the other to mark off the eating space. A runner might mark a 'passage' between two different parts of a room – perhaps a seating arrangement and a study space.

On the wall Rugs make excellent wall hangings, particularly in smaller rooms where, if used in the conventional way, they would be completely hidden by furniture. You can also throw a rug over a sofa or chair or use a thin, flat-woven

Low line

An abstract design in mostly grey and cream accented with black works well in a simple modern living room where most of the interest is kept low by means of the strong horizontal lines of the table and venetian blind.

The black in the rug is repeated in the painted floor, table and accessories.

one as an unusual bed cover.

Practicalities Choosing a large rug to almost fill a room has a number of advantages over a fitting a carpet. It is always more expensive than you anticipate to carpet over all the odd corners of a room and also involves a certain amount of wastage. A big rug can, therefore, be a rather more economical buy.

In addition, a rug can be turned round to even out the wear and can easily be sent away to be cleaned when necessary.

Instead of replacing a fitted carpet which is worn or stained in the centre, you could put a large rug on top.

With a number of rugs, you can rearrange them around the house and, when you move, you simply roll them up and take them with you.

▷ *Focal point*
A large dhurrie in a geometric design holds the main seating area here and forms the focus of a sophisticated modern scheme.

△ *Wood and wool*
Mellow stripped woodwork, floorboards and furniture set off the texture and warmth of a wool rug with rich oriental colouring.

In this dining room of an older house the effect is to isolate the dining table and chairs on a rug island.

▷ *Seating area*
Rugs work well on top of worn, or inexpensive fitted cord carpet. In this case a design has been chosen to define the seating area and to pull together the colour scheme. The warm rusts and beiges and soft blues of the fabrics and the diamond pattern of the wallpaper are picked up by the rug.

◁ **Textural contrast**
The architectural lines of the furniture
and fireplace are counterbalanced by a
stylized floral rug with a feel of the
thirties. The contrast between the
clean-cut shapes and shiny hardness of
the furniture, floor and whole room
below dado height and the soft, deep
pile of the carpet successfully isolates
the dining area.

▽ **Country feel**
Plain white walls are the setting for this
kitchen/dining room. Stripped wood
door and floorboards have been
contrasted with streamlined white and
red units, red hob, sink and venetian
blind.
   The multi-coloured cotton rag rug
blends the two themes; it picks up the
colours of the scheme and echoes the
country feel of the pine and the
Windsor chair.

◁ *Room divider*
The problem with this sitting room is that doors to the two adjoining areas face each other. Through traffic cuts off a narrow section of the room, rendering it useless.

This disadvantage has been turned to good use by accentuating the passageway effects with a runner. On one side is the seating area and on the other a shallow desk creates a small study space. Extra chairs can be drawn into the conversation circle when necessary.

▽ *Wall hanging*
A richly patterned rug makes a dramatic statement in an otherwise neutral interior. Some oriental rugs are fragile and should not be walked on and, in any case, hanging such a rug on a wall shows the design off to advantage.

Oriental carpets such as this give an opulent feel to a room; if you cannot afford a real one, you can achieve the same effect with a less expensive copy.

BRIGHT IDEA

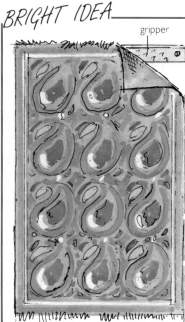

gripper

Hanging a lightweight rug
Screw a piece of carpet gripper strip, very slightly shorter than the rug width, securely to the wall.

Press the rug firmly onto the strip; it will be held in place by the little spikes.

This method is not suitable for fine or large pieces.

The Magic of Plants

Houseplants are one of the quickest and least expensive ways of bringing life and interest to a room. A splash of green instantly revives a rather tired scheme, and flowering plants provide a lively range of colours.

Placing plants There are few design rules about where to put plants – greenery and flowers look good almost anywhere, as long as they are not in the way of everyday activities.

Treat large floor-level plants as focal points, making full use of your lighting to show them off to best effect. Some plants need less light than others, but normal artificial lighting is no substitute for the natural daylight that all plants need.

Medium-sized plants can be placed on furniture, but there are alternatives – hanging baskets, wall-hung planters, stands or window shelves.

Small plants, such as African violets, need placing with care. They usually look and grow best grouped in a box or on a stand.

The right environment Make sure you match a plant to its growing conditions. Cacti and succulents need plenty of direct sunlight; ferns and palms survive in shade. Cyclamen, azaleas and chrysanthemums don't like the atmospheric dryness and levels of warmth found in the average centrally heated room. It helps to stand them on a saucer filled with gravel and keep it topped up.

Maidenhair ferns are delicate and are unsuitable for draughty windows. Begonias hate gas and won't thrive in a kitchen with a gas appliance, although natural gas is less harmful than coal gas.

Bromeliads such as the urn plant, queen's tears, flaming sword and variegated pineapple plant, and epiphytes such as bird's nest fern and many orchids, thrive in the warm, steamy conditions of a bathroom.

◁ *A splash of green*
Plants bring a fresh, lively look to a bathroom and ferns, ivies, bromeliads and epiphytes thrive in low light levels.

△ *Hang it all*
A china hanging basket filled with variegated ivy, tradescantia and polka-dot plants makes an eye-catching replacement for a disused light fitting and saves valuable shelf space.

You can also buy plastic hanging baskets with drip trays attached. Plant trailers round the edge and uprights in the centre.

▷ Living highlights

Plants and flowers help bring the garden indoors and add a human touch to your decorative scheme. The delicate structure of leaves and flowers also helps to soften hard outlines of modern furniture.

Here, the white flowers of these marguerites are perfect for cheering up a shady corner in which a darker plant would go unnoticed. More marguerites repeat the daisy theme in the foreground. With care, and frequent dead heading, they will last a lot longer than cut flowers, as long as they get sufficient sunlight at some time during the day.

◁ Stepping out

Greenhouse staging, painted white or dark green, is perfect for displaying groups of small plants indoors.

Alternatively, you could use a small stepladder or disused trolley. To avoid drips, stand plants in saucers or on shallow, gravel-filled plastic trays and keep permanently moist. Choose plants with a variety of shapes and colours and try to include some trailing plants to break up horizontal lines.

▷ Mutual benefits

This plant stand containing devil's ivy, spider plant and ivy makes a perfect feature for filling an empty spot in the living room, bedroom or hall. Inexpensive bamboo, wicker and rattan plant stands are widely available, both new and second hand.

◁ Unusual containers

Old teapots and jugs can make pretty cache-pots. Fill them with gravel to support plant pots and provide drainage: never plant straight in as the roots become waterlogged.

Decorating with Large Plants

Even a small, humble tradescantia (wandering sailor) can help to bring a room to life, but for maximum impact, invest in one or two large plants. Large plants can be used in many different ways. A leafy specimen placed close to a picture window or patio doors leads the eye to the light and on to a leafy garden or balcony outside. In many houses, rooms are linked by an arch or opening. A plant placed on one side so that it is only partly visible draws the eye from one area to the other.

Choose a plant to complement the style of your room. Palms look well with Art Deco shapes, chrome and glass; the small delicate leaves of *Ficus benjamina* (weeping fig) give a light and airy garden feel to a traditional chintzy setting; and angular yuccas and dracaenas (dragon plants) suit minimalist modern schemes.

A large plant can play a practical as well as a decorative role by helping to fill up space in a sparsely-furnished room. If you position an uplighter below a big plant, the leaves cast interesting shadows on the wall and ceiling. Don't position the lamp too close to the leaves as they could scorch. Plants look good only if they are healthy, so it is worthwhile investing in a good houseplant care book.

A taste of India

Plants combined with rattan furniture, a woodblock floor and pale walls give a colonial feel. A well-shaped palm almost fills one wall and is balanced by an equally tall, but upright, Ficus lyrata *(fiddle-leaf fig) and several* cyperus *(umbrella plants) of varying sizes. The pink* Impatiens *on the table adds a subtle splash of colour.*

Make a bold statement ▷

A single, dramatic plant is used to make a bold focal point in this simple modern room. The spiky leaves of the dracaena (dragon plant) and the shadow it casts echo the bold geometric design of the wall hanging. A yucca or large cyperus (umbrella plant) could be used in the same way.

Green and pleasant ▽

The comfortable feel of this period room owes much to the clever use of plants. A dramatic palm makes the focal point and is complemented by smaller plants and groups of white flowers. A simple colour scheme of white and palest green with the darker green of the plants reflected in pieces of pottery, adds up to a look which is cool and elegant.

Decorating with Dried Flowers

dry day after the dew has evaporated. Strip off the leaves and tie the flowers into small bunches. Hang them upside down in a cool, shady place out of direct sunlight. The best flowers for drying are the 'everlasting' varieties such as helichrysums and statice. Other non-fleshy flowers, golden rod, achillea, gypsophila, lupin, sea holly, delphinium and hydrangea are also suitable for drying by this method.

Dried flower arrangements can be formal or informal to suit the setting. Baskets of flowers are particularly pleasing in a mellow pine kitchen while brass bowls and china containers of blooms complement dark wood furniture and old oil paintings. A large arrangement of dried seed heads and flowers is one of the most attractive ways to fill an empty fireplace.

There is a wide range of dried flowers available in shops, either loose or in a ready-made arrangement, or you can dry your own. Pick the flowers on a

Baskets of bloom
A selection of dried flowers, seed heads and berries massed together in baskets of varying sizes makes a stunning display. Blooms shown here include statice, hydrangea and helichrysum.

One of the simplest ways to display dried flowers is to group them together in a selection of baskets. Massed gypsophila looks good in a big basket, as do hydrangeas or peonies. Smaller baskets can be filled with more delicate blooms, small seed heads and berries. You can change the display to suit the season. Simple bunches of lavender or dried herbs can be hung from beams or from butcher's hooks hanging from a rail or grid. Discard dried flowers when they begin to lose their colour and start to shed petals.

Dried flower arrangements If you want a formal arrangement, flowers can be pushed into flower-arrangers' foam in the same way as fresh blooms. The foam should be left dry. Look for unusual containers to hold the flowers. Old fashioned china tureens, gravy boats, serving dishes and china candy baskets all make an effective and interesting display. Match the colours of the dried flowers to the colours used in the pattern on the china. If you wish, dried flowers can be mixed with fresh foliage, autumn leaves or berries.

△ **An eye for tradition**
This formal arrangement of rosebuds, helichrysum, lavender, hydrangeas and achillea complements the dark wood of the Jacobean-style hall table and provides a visual balance for the large brass Buddha which would otherwise dominate the scene and dwarf the smaller pictures and ornaments.

◁ **Floral focal point**
An old-fashioned china jardinière topped by a display of dried flowers is a charming and effective way to create a focal point. Here, dried peonies and hydrangeas echo the colours of the flowers on the pedestal.

◁ *Fireplace display*
An arrangement of dried flowers is a good way to fill an empty fireplace. The flowers can be arranged in a tall vase, a bowl or in a basket, as shown here. A tall, two-tiered basket, overflowing with dried flowers, fills the space in this large, imposing fireplace. One basket or vase of flowers is sufficient for most fireplaces.

◁ *Natural fragrance*
A bowl of pot pourri adds gentle scent and a spot of subtle colour to a room. A glass bowl shows the petals and herbs to best advantage.

MAKING POT POURRI

Bowls of sweetly scented pot pourri are an attractive variation on the dried flower theme. The flowers used in pot pourri depend on what is available. Rose petals are a good base and can be mixed with lavender or camomile flowers, marigold petals, lemon balm, lemon verbena or lemon geranium leaves. Herbs, such as rosemary and thyme can also be used. Thinly pared orange or lemon peel plus a dash of cinnamon, cloves, or nutmeg add originality.

Gathering and drying Collect your flower petals and scented leaves on a dry day after the dew has evaporated. Dry petals and flower heads in a cool, shady place. This will help the flowers to keep their colour. Put a handful of petals in a brown paper bag. Secure the top with an elastic band and leave the bag in a warm, dry place for two to three days. Shake the bag once a day. When petals become papery, they are ready.

Scented leaves and thinly pared orange and lemon rind can be treated in the same way. Leaves are ready when they become crumbly.

Tie lavender and herbs in bunches and hang them upside down to dry. Remove the flowers and leaves when dry and discard stems.

Fragrant oils and orris root are added to pot pourri to enhance the scent. You can buy ready blended oils or make your own mixture. Orris root powder is added to fix the perfume.

Basic pot pourri Place six teacups of rose petals in a large bowl. Add other petals, leaves and herbs of your choice. Sprinkle on four or five drops of oil then three teaspoonsful of orris root powder. Mix well with your hands. Stir daily for a week.

BRIGHT IDEA

Make a tree Three-quarters fill a flowerpot with interior filler. Insert a piece of dowelling and leave filler to set. Wind ribbon or raffia around the dowelling 'trunk' and stick a Styrofoam ball on to the top.

Cut the stems of small flowers to about 7.5cm. Push the flowers into the ball to make a well-balanced shape.

△ *Kitchen choice*
Fresh flowers quickly wilt and fade in the kitchen but a dried arrangement will withstand steam and heat. This floral tree is easy to make (see Bright Idea, opposite) and looks effective teamed with country style kitchen units. Dried flowers can be hung in bunches from the ceiling or tucked into cane and basketwork – as shown here around the frame of the mirror.

▷ *Balanced arrangement*
The fireplace in this room has been completely removed and the opening turned into an alcove. The space is too large for a simple flower arrangement so a pair of old scales has been used with a bicycle basket filled with dried flowers on one pan and brass weights on the other. An old school clock balances the display.

Display China on Shelves or Hung on Walls

Any collection of china lends itself well to display. It might be a collection of one type of object – a variety of china egg-cups or toast-racks, for example. Or it might be a rich mixture of quite different china objects – perhaps related in shape, colour or style or brought together simply because you like the look of them.

Building up a collection of china can be a lot of fun, too, and it need not be expensive. Junk shops and jumble sales, for example, are good hunting grounds for cheap and cheerful ornaments that can be every bit as effective as antique bone china.

On display China on display generally looks best if it is grouped together, but there's no need to limit the display to china alone. Mixing it with other, quite different things, can provide interesting contrasts of texture and style.

Whatever the display, make sure that you leave enough space so that each piece can be appreciated properly. And remember that the arrangement need not be fixed and static. Moving things round – perhaps even exchanging one or two pieces for different ones – is one of the quickest and least expensive ways of adding a fresh, new look to a room.

Positioning All types of china – from teacups to decorative ornaments – can be placed on almost any sort of ledge, as long as it's not in a vulnerable position. Shelves, open dressers and mantelpieces all fit the bill: glass-fronted cabinets eliminate the need for regular dusting and make ideal showcases for china that is precious.

China plates are, of course, best displayed upright if you are to appreciate their colours and patterns. They make an attractive backdrop to a shelf display, but they can also be hung on walls instead of the usual arrangements of framed pictures.

△ *Wall hanging*
This trio of two wall-hung vases and a painted china plate make a simple and attractive arrangement. The blue and yellow flowers successfully link up three objects with very different shapes and style.

◁ *Shelf display*
This collection of art nouveau china displays a wonderful variety of colour, form and texture.

To prevent plates that are displayed upright from slipping or toppling over, fix a strip of beading to the shelf or cut a shallow groove in the wood.

▷ **Plate arrangement**
Pretty plates – perhaps too old or precious to use – are grouped all over these kitchen walls.

The variations in size and shape make the display more interesting, and the blue-and-white theme is echoed in the matching wall tiles and bright blue wicker chairs.

▽ **Modern lines**
An alcove fitted with built-in shelving provides perfect display for china objects of different shapes and sizes. Here, even the floor of the alcove is put to good use – perfect as long a there are no small children in the house!

The delicate colours and textures of this modern collection are elegantly displayed against pale honey-coloured walls to create maximum impact.

△ **Country cottage china**
These bright and cheerful collections of country cottage china are set off by the white-painted shelving against a soft pink background.

Screw cup hooks into shelves for hanging cups and mugs. To display individual plates, use special plate stands such as those on the bottom shelf – available in wood as well as plastic.

△ Kitchen collection

Kitchen china that can be seen and is easily accessible makes a practical and decorative display. Limit shelving to about 20cm deep for easy reach.

◁ Mantelpieces

A mantelpiece is a prime spot for displaying china to advantage: it is an obvious focal point of the room, and the height of the shelf allows each object to be seen easily.

Here, the pretty shelf collection is loosely arranged, in contrast with the bright blue china horses lined up along a moulding of the fire surround.

▷ **Dresser looks**
A china dinner set that is only used on special occasions makes an attractive and almost permanent display on the painted dresser. Do not aim for a completely symmetrical arrangement – the slightly random look as shown here is more attractive.

▽ **1930s style**
A collection of wall-vases from the art deco period make up a personal collage on these walls and there is space to add to it, from time to time.

The theme is continued with the lamp and figure on the table in front.

BRIGHT IDEA

USEFUL ACCESSORIES
Some plates are intended for wall display and have holes in their base so that they can be hung from a picture hook. For hanging ordinary plates, you can buy special plastic-coated wire plate hooks. Wood or wire plate stands are also available for displaying plates safely in an upright position on a shelf or table.

Table-top Collections

Whether you are an avid collector or merely like to acquire knick-knacks which take your fancy, displaying them attractively enables you not only to enjoy them yourself but to show them off to others as well! A display need not be made up of valuable collectors' items; simple everyday objects – pebbles from the beach together with unusual rocks, perhaps – can be just as pleasing.

A collection of any sort adds individuality to a room – and one displayed on a table rather than hung on the wall is more flexible since you can easily alter the layout or replace some of the items as the fancy takes you.

Arranging the display Although there is no blueprint to success, the best advice is to approach the display as an artist might approach a still-life composition. Scale and proportion are all important. If there is a mixture of sizes, try to balance the large and the small, the tall and the short.

It's often easier to achieve a pleasing display if the objects are linked in some way – by subject, colour, texture or even size. But there is nothing to prevent you from creating a stunning display of items linked by no more than the fact that you like them!

The great blessing of a table-top collection is that if you aren't completely satisfied, you can simply start all over again. Try and try again – until you are completely satisfied with the end result.

A charming miscellany
This idiosyncratic assortment of objects is safely positioned against a wall. A richly-coloured floor-length tablecloth with a matching over-cloth draws attention to the arrangement.

CHOOSING THE TABLE

Above all else, the table should be stable and placed where it won't be bumped into by even the most careless members of the family.

The dimensions of the table should reflect the size of the things to be displayed. A few tiny objects may get lost on a large and imposing table top – conversely, large things may overcrowd a delicate side table. In practice, the only way of finding out whether your choice works is to try it out. A set of tiny thimbles arranged to one side of the top of a large chest of drawers may work well – while the same items seem to disappear if they are more spread out. The smaller the objects, the closer the grouping needs to be so that each piece gains strength from its companion.

▷ *Glass with a brass trim*
Arranging these ceramic ornaments into groups with similar colouring and shape gives a pleasing order to this collection of small objects. Tall candlesticks together with the gilt-framed painting and brass shelf edging frame the collection.

◁ *Peach and leaf green*
Leaves, flowers and budgerigars are the theme of this unusual table-top display. The collection of china with a nature theme is complemented by pot plants and cut flowers.

▽ *A formal note*
Polished wood is the perfect setting for this symmetrical arrangement of china boxes and figurines. The trellis wallpaper is an appropriate backdrop for the flowering jasmine.

Table Settings

It's not necessary to have a vast stock of different china and glass, although, if you can afford it, an everyday plus a 'best' set will give you greater scope. If not, stick to something simple. All-white china or a classic shape in white or cream with just a line of colour around the edge will give scope for a variety of looks. Use plain glasses and add a cloth in a primary colour and checked napkins for an informal lunch, pastel linen and delicate flowers for a summery supper or lace and candles as a setting for dinner.

Table decorations play an important part in creating the style of the setting – fruit, flowers, candles and so on can be chosen to suit the seasons as well as the occasion. Keep central arrangements low or your guests will have trouble talking through it! If you are not using the whole table, you can place the arrangement at one end, if there is sufficient space.

Flowers and fruit

A pastel setting is built around flower-strewn china. The theme is expanded with a frosted fruit and silk flower table centre. The cloth is four quarter circles of fabric in flower shades with ribbon covering joins.

FROSTING FRUIT

It is a simple matter to give fresh fruit a festive sparkle.

To create frosted highlights, brush egg white lightly on to the fruit where required. Then sprinkle with granulated sugar.

For all-over frosting on stemmed fruit, hold the fruit by its stem and dip into the egg white. Turn in granulated sugar to cover, then gently shake off the excess.

▷ *Against the wall*
As the table is pushed against it, the wall here almost becomes part of the setting. Tableware and napkins in an all-over printed design echo the wallpaper's pattern and muted colour. They are set off by tones of plain pink – chairs, cloth and candles.

◁ *Soft elegance*
A setting in pale pink and cream creates a romantic mood and picks up the colouring of trellis wallpaper and painted bamboo furniture. A lace cloth softens the plain one below and candles give a flattering soft light. The arrangement of garden flowers is low enough to allow conversation.

▽ *Versatile white china*
A sophisticated setting where the food is as carefully arranged as the table. The dramatic flower arrangement is the sole indulgence in an almost severe scheme. As it fills the empty sixth place it does not block the diners' view across the table.

A totally different, rustic mood could be created in this plain room by using the same china on a blue and white checked cloth with red cutlery.

Christmas Tables

The decoration on your Christmas table needs to harmonize with the rest of the room. If you have greenery and berries round the room, choose red flowers and red and green ribbons on a white cloth. If you've used silver, gold and glitter again follow the theme. Don't overdo these shiny materials, however, as too much can look rather tawdry.

Adapt your decoration to suit the time of day and the meal. A tea table is simpler and less formal than one set for dinner; a party table for children needs to be eye-catching but robust!

To be attractive, your decorations do not have to be expensive shop-bought ones: something you have made yourself very often has more charm. If you've paid a lot of money for a table centre the temptation is to bring it out year after year. With a home-made one, when Christmas is over you can throw it away and start afresh next year.

▽ *Traditionally new*
The classic red, green and white theme is given a new twist with white cotton and muslin caught up in festoons. Red and green ribbons looped and loosely tied in bows cover the gathers.

△ *Formal fruit and cones*
Brass candlesticks and bronze cutlery add a renaissance air to a formal dinner table. The lemons and cones that make up the centrepiece are divided by gold doilies.

PAPER FLOWERS

Fold a 15×36cm strip of crepe paper in half lengthwise and wind round a flower wire to make a bud and stick. Cut 12 petals, about 10cm long and following the outline above left, from crepe paper. Arrange around the bud, sticking in place as you go. Curl by rolling over a pencil and stretch the top edges to give a realistic appearance. Bind base and stem with florist's stem binding.

Cut out leaves from coloured foil, slightly larger than the petals. Stick together in pairs with a flower wire in between.

△ *In snowy mood*
This unusual scheme for a children's tea echoes the winter landscape. It works because it retains traditional elements such as star-shape biscuits. The table arrangement is an Advent ring.

▽ *Parcel castle*
A red and gold cardboard castle filled with presents is the centrepiece here. Ribbons attached to each parcel run from each place setting. Paper plates and beakers pick up the colour scheme.

Dressing the Table

A carefully-chosen cloth need not only be used to create a well-dressed dinner table by acting as a background for attractive china and glass. It can also play a much more important and permanent role in a room's decoration.

A floor-length cloth on a round display table, for example, can be designed to pick up patterns and colourings used elsewhere in the room, perhaps with a top cloth in an accent colour or a co-ordinating design.

In a rather severe modern dining room with venetian blinds at the window and a large central table, a plain long cloth will provide a softening touch. Square side tables, similarly treated, could serve the same purpose.

The fabric can be used to link differing styles of furniture; a modern, monochrome treatment of a traditional bird or flower design, made up into a simple square or rectangular cloth, helps harmonize modern chairs and antique occasional pieces.

If you are thinking of re-upholstering your furniture or putting up new curtains but are not quite sure about your choice of fabric, you could make a tablecloth from a couple of metres just to see how well the colour and pattern fit into the room. This is a safer bet than buying metres and metres of fabric only to find you've made a mistake.

Tablecloths can also add a real finishing touch to a room scheme when they are used to cover unsightly second-hand tables or cheap, unfinished chipboard display tables.

▽ *Lace topping*
The cloths here – a traditionally patterned lace fabric over a plain cotton – pick up the themes of this room. The undercloth is in the warm, sunny yellow of the walls; the top one complements the lace of the curtains. The fresh green of the shutters, which is picked up in the painted furniture, counterpoints the scheme.

△ *Blue and white style*
The way fabric has been used in this rather stark scheme adds a softening touch without detracting from the stylish appeal of the room. The floor-length tablecloth in a sophisticated geometric batik pattern complements the table's rectangular shape and tones with the fabric used to cover the screen.

◁ *Perfect balance*
In this room, with its strong scheme of blue and white, the table has a floor-length cloth in a pattern to match the wallpaper. To balance the strong design, the pattern elsewhere in the room is reduced to a minimum — even the pictures on the wall are in simple, dark tones. The design of the wallpaper and tablecloth fabric has been highlighted by topping the floor-length cloth with another cloth which matches the brightest blue in the design, while the table stands on a rug of the darkest shade.

▽ **Theme of flowers**
The round table with its double layer of cloths is an integral part of this summery room. The undercloth tones with the colouring of the curtain fabric, while the top cloth picks up the colour of the wall; its applique edge echoes the flowery theme of the other fabrics. The whole arrangement creates interest in an otherwise empty corner.

▽ **The perfect link**
Classic furniture from different periods is linked by the choice and style of tablecovering. The undercloth and matching curtains in a stylized floral pattern complement the side table and armoire while the simple blue and white colourway suits the pure lines of the Bauhaus chairs. The top cloth creates a simple backdrop for the table setting.

Decorative Bedheads

A bedhead makes a dramatic focal point in the bedroom. Some are purely decorative, while others serve a practical purpose as well. Reading or breakfasting in bed is much pleasanter if you have something comfortable to lean on, and a bedhead will also stop pillows from slipping down behind the bed.

There's quite a variety to choose from — including headboards covered in fabric and a hand-decorated wooden bedhead — and all are relatively easy to make.

For greatest comfort, make a bedhead that is padded with wadding or foam and cover it with fabric to match or co-ordinate with the rest of the room.

It's a good idea to choose fabric in a colour that won't show head marks too quickly and that can be sponged clean, or sprayed with a fabric protector such as Scotchgard. A loose cover — slip-over or throwover — is always a practical choice since it can be removed easily for regular washing. Make sure you use a washable Terylene wadding, available in several different thicknesses, to add padding if required.

△ **Cushioned to comfort**
It is easy to hang comfortable cushions with fabric loops from a curtain pole fixed to the wall above head height for sitting up in bed.

Here, a decorative frill with piped trim adds a professional finish.

▽ **Quilted comfort**
A pretty patchwork quilt folded over a pole is one of the simplest ways of making a bedhead. It is padded for comfort and held in place by Velcro strips sewn to the back edges.

▷ **Simple backing**
An eye-catching floral print transforms a humble divan.

The bedhead is made from a piece of chipboard screwed to two wooden battens which are fixed to the divan base. Cover the front and edges of the chipboard with a piece of thin Terylene wadding, and staple or tack it to the back of the board. Then smooth the fabric over the padding and secure with staples or tacks.

▽ **Slip-over cover**
You can give a new look to a plain headboard with a removable, washable cover.

Make the cover on the tea-cosy principle, with plain fabric for the back and padded or quilted fabric on the front. This pretty quilted bedspread is edged with striped fabric for definition.

◁ **Lacy touch**

Antique cotton lace, draped high above a wooden bedhead, is a decorative touch that suits this pretty Victorian room. The swags are crowned with a posy of dried flowers and spread along the picture rail.

▽ **Bed curtains**

These drapes give the graceful effect of a four poster without its bulk.

To make your own, mount a semi-circular chipboard shelf (24mm thick) on the wall with a metal shelf bracket and cover the underside with fabric. Make two curtains from lightweight fabric, gather and fix to edge of shelf with tacks. Cover tacks with braid. Hang the sheer curtain from a curtain pole fixed to the wall.

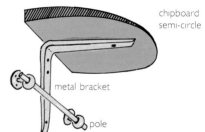

chipboard semi-circle

metal bracket

pole

△ Buttoned up
A deep-buttoned fabric headboard is soft and luxurious. If upholstering your own, choose a simple shape with gentle curves that is easy to cover.

▽ Shelf space
One way to build a bedhead over an old fireplace – the stepped shelving doubles as a bedside table with space for ornaments and flowers.

△ Victorian charm
Flowers and ribbons transform this wooden headboard, and it's easy to achieve the same effect. Buy paper cut-outs made specially for decoupage or cut out suitable designs from a piece of wallpaper. Glue them down, then apply two or three protective coats of clear polyurethane varnish.

Perfect Patchwork

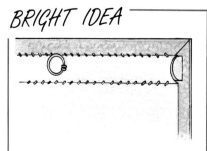

BRIGHT IDEA

HANGING A QUILT
Cut a 25 mm by 6mm batten slightly shorter than the width of the quilt. Using 50mm wide tape, stitch a casing close to the top of the quilt and insert the batten. Sew two curtain rings to the casing 300mm from each end and one in the centre, and hang from picture hooks.

Cheerful, colourful patchwork adds a comforting country air to any room in the house. Use it in the traditional way as a bedcover, or branch out with patchwork cushions, tablecloths, hangings and accessories.

If you are lucky enough to own an original hand-made quilt, the best way to display it is on the wall. Position the quilt where it can be admired, facing seating or a bed. If the quilt is old and valuable, keep it out of direct sunlight as this fades the fabric. A modern quilt, which can stand up to wear and tear, can be thrown over a shabby sofa or chair for an instant facelift. Alternatively, use a piece of ready-quilted fabric.

There is no need to limit yourself to just one big piece of patchwork in a room. Add instant colour and life with a scattering of patchwork cushions – make them yourself in colours to complement your room scheme using a patchwork pieces kit. Skilled sewers can make patchwork lampshades, add a patchwork edging or centrepiece to a tablecloth or stitch placemats to complement china. A patchwork border or edging is also a clever way to lengthen or widen curtains.

Mix and match
You can mix and match patchwork successfully, providing that all the pieces are in similar colours. The quilt on the wall is made in a design called Dresden Plate.

◁ **On display**

If you are lucky enough to own a beautiful original quilt like this wall-hung American pieced design, it can become the centrepoint of a room scheme. The crisp blue and white colouring is complemented by plain soft and dark blue quilts on the bed, and by a paler blue and pink check design on the chaise longue. More patchwork, this time in strong blue-black and white, covers the bedside table. The secret of this successful room scheme is the use of one colour in several shades to unify the mixture of patchwork patterns and shapes.

▷ **Patchwork in paint**

The central cross motif of this simple pale green and rose pink quilt is used again and again in this pretty bedroom. The bed headboard, chest and walls are painted in palest pink, then stencilled with the motif, using a template copied from the quilt. The central wheel motif made up in fabric to match the quilt becomes an attractive framed picture. Simple pink and green quilted cushions complete the scheme.

◁ **The art of disguise**

Upholstered seating which is dull, past its best or in a fabric you hate can be given a new lease of life with patchwork. No sewing skills are needed – just drape the quilt over the sofa or chair for an instant facelift. Patchwork in pale, summery colours gives formal seating the right relaxed comfortable look for this cool, plant-filled garden room. The simple cotton rag rug reflects the patchwork theme.

Cushions for Decoration

Cushions are versatile accessories for any home. Piles of them give a look of inviting comfort to a bedroom or sitting room and can be used to transform a bed into a sofa in a bed-sitting room. As well as the obvious comfort they give they play a valid part in creating a colour scheme.

In many rooms the most dominant pattern appears on the curtain fabric; perhaps a bold floral design with uphol- stery in a single colour. The obvious choice of fabric for cushions is to use that of the curtains to bring the pattern on to sofas and chairs to tie the colour scheme together.

You might also choose cushions in different plain colours to pick up those in the curtains. You could also pick a striped fabric incorporating a selection of the colours for some cushions. This is also an excellent way to echo the colouring of patterned upholstery.

Adding a cushion or two is an inexpensive way to experiment with introducing additional patterns into a room, or to find out if you can live happily with a design. It is also a good way to give an accent of colour to lift an otherwise monotonous scheme.

In adjoining rooms, rather than sla- vishly repeating the colour scheme from one room to the other, you can achieve continuity by a well-chosen mixture of cushions. You could use the fabric of dining room curtains for cushions in a living room opening from it. Or pick up the colour of hall walls in rooms opening from it.

In a monochromatic scheme try to choose lots of cushions in varying textures to give interest.

Fabric and tapestry
Needlepoint cushion in rich blues, reds and pinks echoes the colouring of the rose and peony curtain fabric.

▷ **Middle eastern mood**
This cushion-strewn sofa is a perfect example of how to mix pattern. In this case five different oriental rug designs are counterbalanced by a tapestry featuring an exotic bird.

▽ **Theme of stripes**
The colour scheme in this room has been carefully worked out around a theme of stripes. Plain cushions on a boldly-striped blue and yellow sofa, piped in the alternate colour, exactly match the shades of the sofa. A single hand-worked patterned cushion provides a focal point and gives a change of pace; the crafted look contrasting with the precise machining of the upholstery and other cushions.

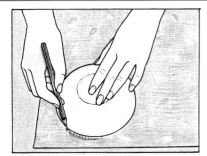

Step 1

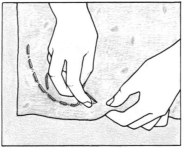

Step 2

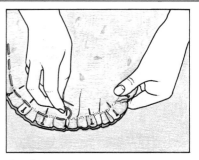

Step 3

EASY CUSHIONS TO MAKE

Simple squashy cushions can be made by curving and gathering the corners of squares or rectangles of fabric and then making up in the usual way.

1. Cut two pieces of fabric to the required size. Then, on the wrong side of one piece, draw an arc in pencil across each corner to join up with the straight side seams. Use a saucer, tea plate or dinner plate as a guide depending on the size of the cushion. Repeat with the other piece of fabric.

2. Hand sew a line of large running stitches around the curve. The aim is to make tucks at the corners rather than fine gathers. Trim off excess fabric across the curve.

3. Pull up and secure the gathering thread to reduce the curve by about half of its length.

4. Place fabric right sides together, tack – paying particular attention to the gathered section – and complete the cushion in the normal way.

Note: You can pipe the edge to give a more tailored look if you wish.

▽ *Strong colours*
Colour and shape are used boldly in this cosy living room. A bright red sofa is covered in equally colourful cushions.

◁ **Adding bolsters**
A gilt Empire sofa calls for a formal treatment. The same stylized Paisley design is used for the sofa itself and the bolsters at each end. Bolsters can be used successfully on a variety of different upholstery styles. Here the bolsters echo perfectly the curls of the arm. Their shape is also perfect for softening the line of rather square furniture.

▽ **White-on-white**
A brass and white-painted iron bedstead is complemented by white-on-white cushions made from old textiles. These cushions are not necessarily expensive. You can make them from the sound sections of old tablecloths or use damask table napkins. Alternatively, piece together scraps of lace.

Bays and Bows

Bay and bow windows can give the effect of living in a goldfish bowl, particularly when the room faces a busy street. It is, therefore, necessary to find a way of giving privacy without blocking out too much light. Curved and angled windows present technical difficulties when deciding how to hang curtains.

Curtains may be hung around the bay to sill or ground length, depending on the style of the room – long curtains being more formal than short ones. If you have a radiator or built-in seat under the window you are limited to short curtains or blinds. Fortunately, there are enough different styles of blind to make windows look tailored, pretty, or grand.

Until recently the only way to hang curtains around a curved or square window was to use flexible track. In some instances the rail incorporates a valance rail to take a frill, giving a softened look. Alternatively, the curtains can be given an attractive heading such as pencil or pinch pleating and hung from a plain track.

It is now possible to buy two different sorts of pole to use in a bay. The first has 'elbows' to join lengths of pole to make up the shape. The second is a system where a continuous brass pole, incorporating a cording action, is bent to suit a particular window.

△ **Maximum light**
A wide square bay has plain white venetian blinds across the front and side windows to filter the sunlight. Only the top portion of the main window is covered; the lower part has glass shelves to add interest.

▽ **Pattern repeat**
Simple, light roller blinds provide shade and privacy, while still allowing light to filter through.

◁ **Breakfast corner**
The bay-shaped window alcove of a basement room has been made into a cosy eating corner with built-in seating following the curve. To avoid covering too much of the small window an austrian blind was chosen. Dress curtains in matching fabric cover the shutters.

▽ **Frill detail**
To give importance to a bay and to add interest to curtains hung from ordinary curved track, a swagged pelmet has been fitted across the whole area. The bound edge of the frill picks up the theme of the frills on the chairs.

△ **Lowering the line**
Roman blinds plus matching full-length curtains have an elegant tailored look which suits these long sashes. The partially-lowered blinds, together with the wide border either side of an unusually high picture rail, visually reduce the height of this tall room.

▷ **Continuous rail**
A brass rail is decorative enough to use without valance or pelmet. This one is specially shaped to fit the bay. Four curtains in the brightest shade of yellow picked from the upholstery fabric are looped back at each end of the bay and at its corners. The curtains are generous enough to draw but roller blinds make it unnecessary to do so.

△ **Light perfection**
Sheer festoon blinds complement this airy room scheme.

▷ **Room without a view**
Removable panels of painted trellis completely cover these windows and hide an unattractive outlook.

MOCK BLIND

You can cover up a window permanently while still allowing it to be easily opened.

You could choose a lightly patterned fabric and stick it to the glass. Alternatively, paint a simple design on to the window with stained-glass paint or cover it with self-adhesive vinyl which looks like stained glass.

Ways with Sheers

Sheer curtains are traditionally used to provide privacy, or to conceal an unattractive view, while still letting in plenty of daylight. Sheers also modify light to a great extent, making it softer and pleasantly diffused.

They have, however, come a long way from the old image of yellowing nets hanging limply from drooping wire. With modern sheer fabrics, and new hanging methods, there are lots of ways of styling them to create attractive window coverings.

Choosing fabric Sheer fabrics, in both natural and synthetic fibres, come in an enormous range of patterns and textures. The choice is anything from traditional floral lace designs to spotted voiles and open geometric weaves for a more modern look.

You can also buy sheer curtains as 'long' and 'short' nets that need very little finishing. Long nets, with decorative selvedges, come in several widths and are sold by the length required. Short nets, with decorative hems, come in standard depths and are sold by the width required.

Most sheer fabrics are either pure white or natural shades, but colours are also available. (You could try dyeing your own.) For the widest choice, look at dress fabrics as well as in the furnishing fabric department.

△ *Cross-over drapes*
Here a single length of striking lacy net transforms a bathroom window. Cross-over drapes look pretty in bedrooms too, and can be put up in a matter of minutes.

For a small window, one width of fabric is usually sufficient so side seams are unnecessary – simply hem the ends. Hang the length of fabric over a wooden curtain pole, arrange it in attractive folds, then catch it back at the sides of the window with a pair of side brackets.

This method of hanging is an excellent solution if you have a piece of real lace that you don't want to cut. If the panel is too long, simply fold it in half before draping it over the pole. Old cords and tassels can be fixed as tiebacks and will complete the effect.

◁ *A simple blind*
A simple roller blind works well on this small window where the fullness of curtain fabric would conceal an attractive frame and sill. The translucent fabric effectively takes the edge off glare, while the blind can easily be adjusted to give varying degrees of light.

A blind is quick and easy to make using a kit, and relatively inexpensive compared to curtains. Most sheer fabrics, even lace, can be used for blinds as long as they are treated with a spray-on stiffening.

◁ *Sheer style*
More imaginative than the usual blind, this creamy sheer drape, with plenty of fullness in it, softens but also enhances the unusual roof angles in this attic bedroom. It is hung with curtain hooks from rings on a pole fixed at the peak of the dormer, and held neatly in place by being looped behind a second pole at sill level.

▽ *A simple heading*
One of the simplest ways of heading sheer curtains is to slide a rod through a casing – any fullness in the fabric will form an attractive ruffle at the top. These curtains cannot be drawn but tiebacks hold them away from the window.

To make a casing, turn over the top of the curtain and machine two rows of stitching to form a channel just wide enough to fit the pole. Elasticated wire is only suitable for the lightest fabrics – it can sag under heavier drapes or across wide windows.

Teaming up △
Crisp broderie anglaise curtains lighten the effect of a plain roller blind, creating a more delicate look for a pretty bedroom.

As the blind can be drawn for privacy, the curtains are purely decorative and therefore not very full. A frilled valance hides the blind when it is not in use.

60

Plug-in Lighting

There's nothing quite so attractive as a room lit by the warm, comfortable glow of table, standard, or floor lamps.

Positioned on low sofa tables, on shelves, a chest, or a sideboard, a table lamp can be used to illuminate a collection, brighten a dark corner, or provide a pool of light for reading. Table lamps come in all shapes, sizes and styles, so it is easy to find something to suit your room. Lamps which beam light downwards and sideways (usually fitted with a wide-based shade) are useful if you want to light a table top or a corner. Vase-shaped uplighters wash light over the wall and ceiling, an attractive way to show off a painting or an interesting architectural feature.

Tall standard lamps look best in a corner or behind a chair. A lamp with a traditional shade, or a shade which covers the top of the bulb, beams down, giving a comfortable pool of light just right for reading. Modern standard lamps are starkly stylish, adding interest to a simple, high-tech look room. Many of these lamps are uplighters and should be positioned so that light washes a wall or the ceiling.

Floor-standing spotlamps look best hidden behind a display of plants so that light shines through the foliage, throwing delicate leaf shadows on ceilings and walls.

Before you buy lamps, look carefully at socket positions. You may need to have extra outlets installed for lamps to be positioned where you want them. Trailing cable is dangerous and tucking cable underneath a carpet or rug can cause a fire.

Always have new sockets installed by a professional electrician.

A pool of light
A table lamp with conical shade beams light down, adding instant interest and comfort to a corner. This type of light is the ideal way to illuminate a collection of small boxes, plates or figures arranged on a table, or on a display cabinet as shown here.

◁ Hidden assets
A chrome floor-mounted uplighter placed below a pair of glass tables adds life and interest to an otherwise dull corner. This type of light can be used to beam through large plants.

△ Lights fantastic
Standard lamps combined with recessed ceiling lighting are perfect for this sophisticated room. Floor-standing reading lamps can be angled to suit people using the sofa.

▷ And so to bed . . .
The perfect bedside lamp beams light over just half of the bed, so that one partner can read while the other sleeps. Lamps should be tall enough so that the light falls in exactly the right position for reading but not so that the beam hits the reader in the eye.

These two stylish examples are exactly right and tall enough for the shade to be safely out of the way of books and other bedside clutter.

Display Lighting

With forethought and planning, display lighting can be simple to install. First decide *what* you want to display, and *where* it is to be positioned. Utilize recesses on either side of a fireplace and tables in the corner of a room. Use walls for small collectables as well as pictures and prints. Don't let displays interfere with main traffic areas, focus interest on wasted spaces instead. Vary levels of illumination and concentrate light over small areas to add drama.

With clever lighting, displays of sentimental junk can become important, precious objects appear to their best advantage, and textures and colours can be emphasized. Different effects are achieved by altering the position of the light source in relation to the object on display, and the type of light used.

Backlighting throws objects into semi-silhouette, while glass appears to glow.

Display lighting can be concealed or be part of the display itself. Shelves are usually lit with a tungsten filament or fluorescent tube hidden behind a baffle. A recessed downlighter concealed behind a fascia at the top of a run of shelves will provide a more defined beam of light. Sophisticated low voltage cabinet lights are available from specialist shops but remember to leave room for the transformer. Table-top displays are often grouped around a lamp, which can either be in sympathy or act as an accent to the display.

Lighting for valuable pictures and old fabrics should not cause fading or discoloration and plants should not be subjected to excessive heat.

△ **Concealed lighting**
Concealed tungsten strips light the collection of crockery and the work surface, punctuating the run of kitchen units. The pale paint finish helps reflect the light.

▽ **Illuminated corner**
The table display is backlit and thrown into semi-silhouette by the lamp, while the translucent shade emits a warm glow over the two prints and casts light up towards the ceiling.

△ **Multiple light sources**
An eyeball downlighter is directed on to the wall, the plant is backlit by an uplighter and the sofa table displays are grouped around simple ceramic lamps.

◁ **Traditional picture lights**
The most foolproof and efficient way of illuminating paintings eliminates glare and shadows caused by frames.

▽ **Tungsten halogen task lighting**
Localized, intense light and strong shadows emphasize the sculptural qualities of the display.

Winter Fireplaces

The fireplace and its surrounding area plays a large part in creating the mood of the room. Take your cue from the fireplace itself when deciding how to treat the wall, mantelpiece and hearth.

A classic marble surround calls for a formal treatment: an imposing fire-basket, with brass fender, fire dogs and implements on the same grand scale. Above it the same formal mood should prevail: a regular grouping of pictures, all of one type, or a large gilt mirror,

with a symmetrical arrangement of objects on the mantelpiece itself. On the other hand, a cottagey brick fireplace is complemented by a willow log basket and rustic iron implements. The same informality affects the choice of pictures and objects.

Ancient and modern
A well-lit formal group of a modern painting and ethnic objects contrasts with an Edwardian fireplace.

FOUR-SIDED LIGHT BEAM
In a fairly large, high-ceilinged room, a sharp beam of light with square or sloping sides as in the picture below, can be created with a special surface or track-mounted spotlight with a framing projector attachment. Always buy from a lighting specialist where fittings are demonstrated.

△ Informal brick
An interesting collection of cottagey pictures and bric-a-brac adds seemingly casual charm to this arched rustic brick fireplace.

▷ Classic elegance
A club fender and an elegant mirror reflecting candle lamps make a formal arrangement to suit this classic hearth.

▽ Modern simplicity
Combine a black cast iron stove with sleek, unobtrusive tiling, modern pictures and streamlined furniture for a touch of Scandinavian simplicity.

Broken Colour Paint Finishes

Ragging and rag-rolling use bunched up rags to break up and lift off wet paint, producing a loose overall pattern rather like crushed velvet. This is simple to do but you have to work fast to treat the paint before it dries: when covering a large area such as a wall it helps if there are two of you working together.

Paints to work with Sponging is easiest with water-based emulsion paints. However, you can use oil-based eggshell paint for a crisper, stronger-coloured

Pale and interesting

Ragging makes such a definite pattern that you can achieve striking effects with quite muted colours. Here, this ragged finish – using a pale shade of blue over a white base – creates a visually interesting but relaxing background for a pretty bedroom.

The flat blue fabric for curtains and bedding emphasizes the soft, broken colour on the walls.

Different paint techniques can be used to create a wonderful variety of textured effects, and they offer an exciting alternative to plain, painted walls or wallpaper.

On the practical side, the soft effect of broken colour is often more flattering to a room than an expanse of solid colour and most finishes will help to disguise rough plaster walls and minor blemishes on woodwork. Dirt marks tend to show up less too.

Broken colour techniques This chapter looks at some of the effects you can create by sponging, ragging and rag-rolling with different colours.

Sponging is easy because you simply dab on one or more colours to create a pretty mottled finish, and the overall colour effect is built up gradually.

mottle, while a tinted oil glaze will give soft, translucent prints.

For ragging and rag-rolling, it's best to use an oil glaze. This is slow drying so that you have plenty of time to work on the finish, and it holds a pattern of rag prints distinctly.

As far as the base coat goes, the general rule is to use oil-based eggshell paint under glaze or eggshell; emulsion under top coats of emulsion.

Materials For sponging, a natural sea sponge produces a soft, irregular mottled effect, while a synthetic one gives a crisp, even finish. You can also sponge on paint with a crumpled cloth for a simple ragged effect. For ragging and rag-rolling, you need a good supply of lint-free rags.

It is a good idea to experiment with different colour combinations and to practise the techniques on spare board or card pre-painted with your base coat until you get the right effect.

▷ *A bold finish*
Ragging, along with rag-rolling, is one of the most dramatic finishes when used with bold combinations of colour. Here a pale mushroom background is ragged with a deep rose pink, and light touches of white and grey are sponged on top using a rag, to give an overall pattern of soft crumpled velvet.

The rose pink colour is repeated below the dado.

◁ *Water colours*
A cool turquoise rag-rolled finish works well with bright white tiles and, combined with mirrors, helps to give this small bathroom a feeling of space.

Rag-rolling involves movement so it's best confined to large, straightforward surfaces such as walls; smaller areas – these window frames, for example – can be 'sponged' with a rag to match.

▷ *Blue-on-white*
This mixture of deep blue sponged on to white looks fresh and sharp. The bath panel is also carefully sponged for a smart co-ordinated look.

Sponging with one colour looks best if it's fairly regular, so spend a little time going over patches of thick colour to even out the effect.

◁ **Bright all over**
Here a clever mix of warm, earthy colours, with cool splashes of blue-grey for contrast, is sponged over walls and ceiling: the result is strong and vivid but not overpowering.

Sponging in two or more colours works best with the lighter colour sponged last: remember to space your first prints so that there's room to fill in the other colours.

△ **Stoney look**
Walls and skirting are lightly sponged in two shades of soft coffee-brown emulsion over a cream base, imitating the mottled appearance of a polished pebble.

The overall effect is cool and uncompetitive.

BRIGHT IDEA

LEAF PATTERN

This plain wooden tray is sponged with a decorative swirl of leaves, with a few touches of gold felt pen added.

To get the same effect, apply primer to bare wood, then two or three coats of emulsion or eggshell paint: rub down between coats using fine wet-and-dry paper with soap and water to prevent scratches.

Cut a simple shape from foam sponge with a sharp craft knife and a pair of scissors. Apply the decorative layer of paint, then a coat or two of clear varnish to protect it.

Painted Woodwork

There is no rule which says you must paint woodwork white, or strip it, or colour it to merge with the walls.

In a room whose walls, window frames and doors are in the same neutral colour, you could paint the skirting board a clear contrasting colour. This will define the line between floor and walls.

You can enliven plain, flat walls by adding mouldings so as to create panels. Use a heavy moulding and drag the walls and woodwork in the same colours to give a grand 18th-century feel. For a more modest effect, use simple beading instead; paint walls a flat pale colour and beading and skirting to contrast.

On a stepped cornice you could use more than one colour; choose colours on the same side of the colour wheel – say blue and green, or apricot and peach. A dragged or washed finish gives a more subtle effect than a solid colour.

Built-in furniture – cupboards, dressers, radiator covers – can be given greater importance with paint. Give a radiator housing the look of marble or stone or make a dresser more interesting by painting it in contrasting colours.

▽ **In the grand manner**
A plain room has been given a grand look by dividing the walls into panels with beading. Pastel blue paint has been unevenly dragged over a creamy base coat. The wet top coat has then been wiped off raised surfaces.

△ **Simply effective**
A simple way to give smooth walls a modern panelled effect is to stick on pre-cut and mitred mouldings. Bright coral paint picks up the colour of the woodwork and contrasts well with the flat-painted creamy walls.

△ Paint effect

An imposing cornice is given definition and impact by using two colours – blue and green. A contrasting raspberry picture rail adds further interest to cream walls. The top coat is washed on to cornice and rail and the walls are rag rolled; these broken finishes give a softer effect than solid colour.

▽ Stone finish

A built-in unit to house a radiator is given the appearance of golden marble with ginger paint dabbed on with a rag over a pale yellow base coat. Maple-framed pictures above echo the colouring of the finish. This treatment would be equally effective on a plainer housing with a brass mesh front, or simple shelf.

△ Built-in dresser

Paint in strongly-contrasting colours makes a pleasant alternative to stripped wood for a dresser. The door frames are in the same green as the skirting and trolley and pick up the wallpaper colour. The architrave and panel beading are in bright corally red. Door panels and chair in a much paler green stop the effect being too heavy.

Plain and Simple Painted Furniture

Secondhand wooden furniture is a sensible, economical choice if your budget is limited or if you have small children. Wooden furniture in good condition looks attractive if it is simply cleaned and polished. Scratched, stained or discoloured pieces can be given a new lease of life with a simple coat of paint. Choose a colour to either complement existing decoration, add a bright splash of accent or provide a contrast.

A painted dining table and chairs work particularly well in a kitchen or family dining room. In such a setting you have scope for imaginative and cheerful colour treatments. You could pick up four bright shades from a blind and use one for each of a set of dining chairs. Or, perhaps, paint the seat, uprights, rails and back struts of each chair in different combinations of all four colours.

In a child's room you could paint each drawer of a white chest in a different colour — blue for socks, red for sweaters and so on — as a fun way to encourage tidiness.

If the room is for an adult, adopt a more sophisticated approach using subtle colours. A utilitarian cupboard can be given a more elegant look by adding fake panels using moulding. Paint the moulding in a contrasting or complementary colour. Moulding can also be added to the doors of bedside tables.

Paint will give your furniture a protective surface which copes well with knocks and spills. When the surface becomes damaged, or you grow tired of the colour, it is a simple matter to repaint the piece.

Party pieces

Ordinary cane seats pick up colours from fabrics and wallcovering in this pastel-coloured dining room. For a tea party the theme is carried even further with beribboned balloons and gaily-wrapped parcels.

▷ **Attracting attention**
Brightly-painted chairs are the focal point of this kitchen/dining room. Four colours – red, blue, yellow and green – have been used in different combinations on each one.

▽ **Panel effect**
This old chest-of-drawers has been painted in one of the colours used to spatter the walls. The chest has been given a coat of eggshell paint in a soft spring green, then 'panels' have been added using a white outline. Knobs are painted to match.

BRIGHT IDEA

Painted lines A plain drawer or door can be given a panel effect with a contrasting painted line.

Draw in the rectangular shape using a soft pencil. Now curve the corners. Make a template for the curve and position it in one corner of the rectangle and hold it in place on the straight edges using masking tape. Using a small brush, paint carefully round the curved edge up to the pencilled line. Repeat with other corners.

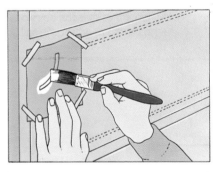

When totally dry, mask off either side of the pencil lines, leaving a small space between of about 2mm.

Paint over the line, leave to dry and remove masking tape. When quite dry remove tape.

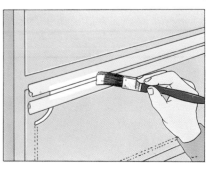

Ways with Old Chairs

Dining chairs dating from the Victorian period and after are in plentiful supply at junk shops and auctions so prices are usually low. Provided that the chairs are free from woodworm and that the frame is in reasonable condition, they can easily be given a brand new look. Look for chairs with interesting moulding and carving as this allows you to pick out details in a contrasting or complementary colour.

When choosing chairs with upholstered seats, look for examples where the seat is intact. A sagging seat needs re-upholstering which is quite a tricky job.

Begin by checking the frame. If the joints of a chair have worked loose, they should be knocked apart and cleaned, then re-glued and clamped until the glue has set.

The next step is to strip the chair of old varnish. You can do this with paint stripper or try a mixture of meths and thinners applied with fine wire wool. This is just as effective as paint stripper and not as unpleasant to use. Wash the chair frame after stripping to neutralize the stripper, sand lightly, then apply a coat of primer. This is essential otherwise the top coat will not cling. You can paint the chairs using satin or high gloss paint, or eggshell – which is an oil-based paint with a matt finish. Acrylic paint (sold in tubes at art shops) is also suitable and is very easy to apply. Tinted or natural wood stains allow the grain of the timber to show through but are only worth applying if the wood is in good condition, as the stain will not hide imperfections.

Choose the fabric for covering chair seats first, then choose the colours for the frame. These can be either contrasting or complementary.

To paint a chair with a drop-in seat, lift the seat out of the chair frame. To re-cover the seats of the three plain chairs, stretch fabric of your choice tightly over the old seat, mitring at the corners for a neat fit. Tack or staple to the underside and return the seat to the chair.

To stencil a chair as pictured, overleaf, rub white emulsion paint into the wood using a cloth. When it is dry, apply a very pale green matt vinyl emulsion. Use a dry brush and apply the emulsion sparingly so that you get a patchy, faded-wood effect. You will need to wipe the brush from time to time to keep it clean.

Use stencil crayons to pattern the chair – a simple design, such as the leaves on the chair overleaf, works best. Apply pattern at random and vary the intensity of colour. Leave the stencilling to dry for two days, then seal with at least two coats of clear polyurethane varnish.

◁ *The plain chair*
Strip, sand and prime the chair. Paint it in just one colour, using eggshell paint which gives a matt finish, or pick out details on the legs and back in another shade, as shown. Cover the seat in a complementary or contrasting fabric.

▽ *The original chairs*
The chairs were selected from this junk shop line-up. Similar models can be found at very low cost. Make sure that frames are free from woodworm and that the seats are intact.

△ **Two shades for success**
Strip, sand and prime the chairs. As this chair has plain paintwork, scratches and imperfections may show up, so fill them with white interior filler. Sand smooth. Paint the main part of the chair in a satin gloss paint to match your chosen fabric and the fancy centre section in a contrasting or complementary colour. Re-cover the seat as described on the previous page.

▷ **Stencil style**
Stencilling looks attractive and is easy if you use stencil crayons. The chair must be stripped and sanded first, then given a base coat of emulsion before stencilling.

△ **The covered chair**
A tailored cover turned this imitation leather 1950s-style chair into an elegant piece of furniture. You can make the cover in plain, even-weave linen or use a furnishing fabric to co-ordinate with curtains or other upholstery. The cover can be removed for cleaning. If using a patterned fabric, be sure to allow enough fabric for the pattern to match at sides.

Designing with Stencils

Stencilling is an ancient technique which was taken from Europe to America by the early settlers and it has become part of that nation's folk art.

As wallpaper became more popular so stencilling declined, but recently there has been a revival of interest and there is a wide range of ready-made stencils. You can also make your own designs, getting ideas from wallpaper books.

Characterless rooms with bare expanses of wall can be made interesting with stencilled panels or you can use stencils for decoration in much the same way as a wallpaper border – at cornice level or immediately above the skirting.

A stencilled border at picture or dado rail level is a clever way to break up the walls of a high-ceilinged room – it will make the ceiling appear lower. You can also emphasize the good features of a room – perhaps by outlining an attractive arch or stencilling a swag above a pretty window.

▽ *Picking up a motif*
Some motifs call for an informal treatment. Here butterflies from the pattern of the fabric are rearranged in flights. Try out the positions of random groupings on a large sheet of newspaper before you start to stencil the wall.

Above are two motifs for you to trace and enlarge; the paint has been smudged sparingly for a subtle effect.

△ **Dresser surround**
A stencilled garland of flowers and fruit outlines a dresser and picks up the colours of the china on the shelves. Three ready-made stencil patterns combine to make up the top 'bar', corner 'knot' and pendant.

◁ **Climbing roses**
A trellis with climbing roses is stencilled over the arch to link this hall and stairway. The motif is taken from the fabric of the tablecloth and lampshade.

▽ **Decorative door panels**
These bedroom walls and cupboards are painted cream and a border design of a spray of flowers runs round the cornice and cupboard doors. The edges of the doors are finished in beading which frames the stencils.

Wallpaper Borders

Wallpaper borders provide tremendous scope for decorating. A splash of pattern adds eye-catching interest to plain walls, while a patterned border can be combined with patterned wallpaper to create a well-finished effect.

Visual trickery Borders are particularly useful for dividing up a lot of blank wall space, and are a good solution if you need to alter the proportions of a room visually.

They can be run along the top edge of a wall as a substitute for a cornice – or used instead of a picture rail or dado. If a ceiling is very high, position a border at picture-rail height and decorate the wall above the same as the ceiling. And a border can be used as a divider to give a neat edge between different finishes and colours.

You can mix and match borders too – use one at cornice level and a second at dado-rail height, for example. To make it easy, many borders are available in co-ordinated ranges which include wallpapers and sometimes fabrics.

Choosing a border There are wide borders and narrow ones, in geometric and floral patterns as well as plain colours. You can even make your own border from a wallpaper with a striped design; cut strips using a straight edge and sharp scissors or a craft knife.

▷ *Baby ducks*
This bold motif matches the paper in colour and tone but works on a larger scale. Strips of hearts, trimmed from the edge of the border, are used to outline the tiled area and panelled cupboards.

▽ *Rose border*
A pretty printed border gives this low-sloping room definition, and adds a splash of pattern to plain, painted walls. The same pattern is used on the bedlinen and for the curtain tiebacks.

△ Dividing line

Part of a beautifully co-ordinated range of paper and fabric, this blue-and-yellow border at picture rail height links the two contrasting wallpapers. Depending on the height of your walls, a picture rail should be between 30 and 45cm below the ceiling. Pin a strip in place to check the position visually.

Note how the cornice has been picked out in blue to add definition to the decorations.

△ Flowered edge

These trailing flowers make an attractive feature of the doorway. Continued along the dado rail, the border plays up the dividing line between different finishes – sprigged wallpaper above, plain pink paint below.

◁ Panel games

A wallpaper border, used to create a decorative panel, cleverly focuses attention on a picture in a large space. Or use the border itself as a frame round a picture or mirror by placing it close to the edge.

You can also divide up a large wall with a series of bordered panels.

Clever Division with Dados

ADDING A DADO RAIL

Rail height The usual height for a dado rail is 90cm from the floor – about one third of the measurement from the floor to the picture rail in a high ceilinged room. If the room is very high, add a picture rail about 30cm below ceiling level. In a room with a ceiling of average height and no picture rail, the dado rail should be fixed about one third of the way up the wall.

Visual effect A dado rail does not always work well in a modern, low-ceilinged room, so try the effect by running a piece of tape or wide ribbon across the wall before you go to the expense of buying rails.

Originally called a chair rail (because it prevented the backs of chairs from banging against the wall and damaging decoration) a dado rail is a length of ornamental wood, plaster or plastic which is fixed across walls to divide the height.

The area between the dado rail and the skirting board is called the dado. In the 18th and 19th centuries, this space was usually covered with a hard wearing material, such as wood panelling or a heavily embossed wallcovering. In the 50s and early 60s, it was fashionable to remove dado rails, leaving blank areas of wall.

These days, dado rails are back in favour and are an ideal starting point for a scheme which involves the use of plain and pattern together, two colours, or for dividing a large and a small pattern, From a purely practical point of view, a dado rail is ideal for dividing the wall in an area where the bottom half of the wall is subject to knocks as all you need to do is redecorate the lower half as needed.

You'll also find a dado rail a useful, easy way to lower the height of a high-ceilinged room. Paint or wallpaper the area below the dado in a dark colour and the area above light. Dado rails can be bought from DIY stores.

A wallpaper border can be used to give a rail effect. Choose a border from a co-ordinated collection and mixing colour and pattern becomes simple, or use the border to divide a paint effect, such as marbling or sponging, from plain paintwork above.

▽ *Divide and rule*
The use of both dado rail and cornice in this dining room means that warm, sunny yellow can be mixed effectively with paler primrose and plain white to divide the wall space visually and add interest. Imagine this same room with plain, one-colour walls and ceiling and you can see why the dado rail is so useful and effective.

△ In traditional style

This Edwardian hallway shows a dado rail used in the traditional way, with heavily embossed wallcovering below, painted in hard-wearing gloss paint, and a more delicate, patterned design above. White paint links the dado rail with the other woodwork and reflects light from the front door.

The wine-coloured wallcovering and leafy green plants complement the colours used in the stained glass door panel. When a dado rail is used in a hallway, it is usually carried on up the staircase and first floor landing and the same decorative treatment is used.

◁ Mix and match

Using a dado rail allows you to use two designs from a co-ordinated collection on one wall. Here both a dado rail and a border divide an abstract and a floral pattern, both taken from the same collection. The border is used above the dado, along the top of the wall and around the under-stairs alcove, drawing attention to the stronger line of the wood rail.

When using co-ordinated collections, use the strongest pattern below the dado rail and match it to curtains, cushions and other accessories. Here, wallcovering has been used on the central panels of the small cupboard doors – a clever touch which completes the scheme.

▷ Low level interest

This elegant room illustrates the original purpose of dado or chair rails, which was to keep the back of the sofa from touching the wall. The dusty pink colour used beneath the dado rail and the rug in front provide a 'frame' for the patterned sofa.

If you have furniture covered in patterned fabric, always keep the area below the dado plain to avoid a space restricting jumble of colour at floor level. A striped border used above the dado rail echoes the colours used in the fabric and wallcovering.

▽ Linking schemes

A border of butterflies and flowers in cool blue-green and white is used as a 'dado rail' to link this bedroom and landing. Plain blue is used below the border on the landing to complement the pretty small print wallcovering used in the bedroom beyond. The same colour is used on the skirting, window frame and other woodwork to reinforce the link between the two rooms.

BRIGHT IDEA

Divide with tiles A row of border tiles used just under halfway up the wall lowers the ceiling and makes a tall, chilly bathroom seem smaller and warmer. There are many tile collections featuring a patterned tile, matching border tile and plain one for use above.

If the walls are already tiled, it may be possible to remove the centre row and add co-ordinating border tiles. Alternatively, remove the bottom half of the tiles and re-tile with patterned tiles and a border, or simply cover the old tiles with new. Ridge the adhesive to make them cling sufficiently.

▷ Back to the wood
If you are stripping doors, window frames and other woodwork, strip the dado rail to match or fit a new rail and stain it to the same shade as the rest of the wood. Stripped wood looks best with country-style patterned wallcovering. Here, a floral stripe is used below the dado rail with a larger version of the same flowers above. The curtains are in matching fabric.

▽ Make a bold statement
Although this dramatic black-and-white striped wallcovering would look effective used alone, the addition of a plain black dado rail to match the table, floor tiles and other woodwork adds impact. Bright, scarlet anthuriums bring a splash of warmth to the room.

▽ Mixing old and new
This old polished chest seems an unlikely partner for modern metal framed pictures and a stylish lamp, yet the scheme works well. The secret of success is the dado rail which adds a touch of tradition and divides the picture frames from the mellow wood.

Crafty Claddings

Creatively used, tongued-and-grooved wood panelling can play many practical and decorative roles in the home.

Tongued-and-grooved panelling provides a useful solution to problem walls. An uneven wall can be straightened, and the cost of renewing the plaster on rough walls can be saved. Similarly, tongued-and-grooved panelling can hide ugly pipes, wires and meters, box in a bath, and even lower high ceilings.

Panelling can also effectively alter the visual proportions of a room. Boards placed horizontally make small rooms feel wider and longer; vertical panelling gives the optical illusion of making low ceilings appear higher. And, of course, it need not cover the entire wall; panelling up to dado height helps to break up high narrow spaces such as hallways as well as protecting the walls from scuffs and scrapes.

In order to show off the beauty inherent in the grain of the wood, tongued-and-grooved panelling can be left in its natural state, protected by a coat of clear varnish. Alternatively, it can be stained, painted, dragged, rag rolled or varnished in a colour.

Fresh blue

Vertical boarding covers the walls of this kitchen to above shoulder height. Instead of finishing the edges with moulding trim, narrow shelves display a collection of china. Painting the boarding, shelves and dresser the same shade of blue gives a feeling of unity.

STAINING PANELLING

Staining new wood is much quicker than painting, but the finished result can look uneven as stain can take quite differently on the end grain and around knots.

Most wood staining products are solvent-based and limited to natural wood colours. Water-based wood stains are easier to use, and a few ranges include primary colours. Cold water fabric dye powders diluted in water are fine for staining small areas, or if you are aiming for a faded 'antique' look. Since fabric dyes are not formulated for wood, they may fade if used on panelling which receives direct sunlight.

▽ Subtle shades

As an alternative finish to sealed natural wood, this panelling has been given an attractive faded look by staining with diluted cold water fabric dye. Squiggles were applied in concentrated dye, and then varnished for protection.

Applying a pattern For the colour on the panelling in the picture below a cold water fabric dye was used to create a subtle faded look. (Alternatives include diluted emulsion paint or wood stain – but do experiment first to test the effect.)

Dilute a small tin of dye with 1.4 litres of water. Brush the solution well into clean, smooth new wood and allow it to dry fully before applying a thin coat of matt polyurethane varnish.

When dry, paint the squiggles. Use a No. 4 artist's brush and cold water fabric dye in a matching or contrasting colour. Mix a bit of dye powder with a little water to get a strong solution. It helps to practise squiggles first until you can draw them with a single stroke. Don't overload the paint brush and keep some kitchen paper handy for blotting up drips. When you are happy with the result, seal with two coats of matt polyurethane varnish when dry.

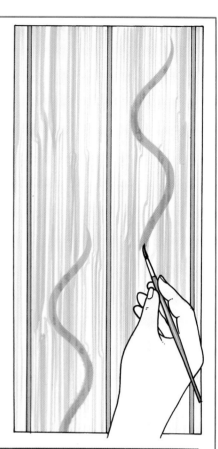

△ **Wavy line**
Tongued-and-grooved boarding painted with gloss paint replaces tiles around the bath to great effect. The boards are high enough to contain shower splashes at one end but have been pre-cut to sweep down in an elegant curve along the side of the bath. The top edge is neatened with flexible plastic strip.

◁ **Topping boards with moulding**
The top edge of tongued-and-grooved panelling can be neatened with a traditional Victorian-style wooden dado rail glued and pinned to the boards. A dado like this is excellent protection for narrow hallways and small utility areas where walls are likely to be knocked.

The vertical grooves in the panelling echo the vertical lines of the old-fashioned cast iron radiator.

△ **Pine kitchen**
Tongued-and-grooved boards fixed horizontally to the walls can make a small kitchen seem visually longer and wider. Wall cladding can also box in unsightly pipework and wiring and provide a neat home for the fridge and cooker. Boards finished with a tough polyurethane varnish need very little looking after.

▷ **Shades of pink**
Tongued-and-grooved boards of varying widths are used for this delicate Victorian-style bedroom. The dado edging is made from a thick nosing combined with narrow beading which continues in a neat line with the window sill. An alternative dado treatment might be to rag roll or drag the dado boards, using the same colour as the walls.

Ways with Wall Tiles

Ceramic tiles are the perfect choice for kitchen and bathroom walls. They won't peel away from the wall or discolour – no matter how steamy the room – and come in colours and shapes to suit all styles of kitchen unit and bathroom sanitaryware.

Major tile manufacturers offer excellent co-ordinated ranges so that you can successfully mix and match a border, a main body pattern and a patterned inset.

Borders and patterned tiles can be used to create panels of pattern in a wall of plain tiling. Make a rectangle of border tiles and fill the centre with pattern. Many tile ranges feature murals, a picture made up of six, eight, ten, twelve, or more tiles which can be used to add colour and interest to a large plain wall.

There's no need to stick to tiles that match. A collection of Victorian tiles makes a glorious jumble of pattern and colour. If you haven't enough to fill the wall, space them out with plains in complementary colours.

DIAGONAL TILING
Wall tiles look effective fixed diagonally, especially if you use alternate stripes of colour, or graduated colours, starting with pale and working up to dark (or vice versa).

Start in a corner, using a set square to find the first true diagonal. Mark the wall into diagonal stripes the width of the tiles you plan to use. Centre a tile on the true diagonal line, then fill in the space below and at either side with cut tiles. Continue until the wall is covered.

Something old...
Colourful Victorian and Edwardian tiles make a stunning surround and splashback in this unusually-shaped bathroom. Note how dark, fairly plain tiles have been used to make a mock skirting board around the bottom of the bath.

MAKE YOUR OWN MOSAIC
Old tiles need not be in good condition to be of interest. Broken pieces can be used to make a colourful tile mosaic. Tile the wall in the normal way, but leave a section bare (how big depends on how many broken pieces you have). Spread tile cement thickly on the bare section, then arrange the broken pieces of tile in a decorative mosaic.

△ *Formal but fun*
Tiles with an informal pattern, such as these cheerful cherries, can be arranged in a formal chessboard pattern with complementary plain tiles to add a touch of style to a splashback or a worktop. Alternatively, arrange the patterned tiles in a row to make a border with the plains below.

▷ *On the border*
Patterned tiles can be used with plains or with complementary patterns below them to create an interesting border effect. Choose a tile with a pattern towards the top, or look for a tile range which features a custom-designed border tile. These are available in both modern and classic styles.

△ In the picture

Unusual picture tiles, like the charming animals, birds and desert scene featured above, are expensive so mix them with budget-priced plain tiles for a clever effect at a sensible price. Here matching plain tiles are used on the worktop and the walls for a smart, practical effect.

▷ 3D drama

Three-dimensional profile tiles make a dramatic frame for a mirror – and can be used to make a mock dado rail half way up a large wall of plain tiling. You can achieve the same effect with trompe l'oeil border tiles.

◁ Plain and simple

Brick-shaped tiles are unusual and effective, especially if you add an interesting geometric design in a contrasting colour, as shown here. Colour could also be added in stripes or squares, depending on the wall size.

Tiling with a difference

△ **Tiling with a difference**
Plain tiles fixed diagonally are more interesting on a large area than conventional tiling, especially if you add a patterned inset.

▽ **Clever deception**
This striped tile design is cleverly patterned so that the tiles look as if they have been fixed to the wall in diagonal lines.

FIXING DIAGONAL TILES

1. Find the true diagonal and mark the wall into stripes.

2. Centre the first tile on the true diagonal.

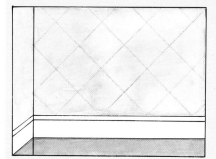

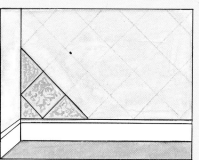

3. Fill in below and at the sides with tiles cut as necessary.

4. Continue building up tiles in diagonal lines across the wall.

Screens as Decoration

Even the most carefully thought-out room may need something extra to pull the various elements together or to give added impact. Screens – often viewed solely as room dividers or as a means of hiding messy corners – can take on an important role in a decorative scheme.

A pictorial screen, painted with a realistic trompe l'oeil sunny view can add to the continental outdoor mood of a room with tiled floor and clean-cut metal and canvas furniture.

A more down-to-earth way to achieve a Mediterranean feel is to sponge a homemade hardboard screen in yellow and blue and set it on white painted floorboards in a room with a summery scheme built round the same clear pastels. Alternatively, you could paint a similar home-made screen with nursery rhyme characters, cars, animals, or seaside scenes to hide the clutter in a child's room.

Many traditional furnishing fabrics have an eastern origin; combine these with mahogany furniture and add an oriental screen to create an 18th-century feel.

Fabric-covered screens have a rather different impact on a room from painted, lacquer, or wood ones. The effect is altogether softer. They sometimes have shaped tops, are padded and covered in chintz.

In a modern setting, however, a much plainer approach works well. Panels of self-coloured woven fabric fixed to a bamboo frame can be most effective. Fabric can also be ruched on to a simple framework; printed fabric will need lining if the back is to be seen. If the room is small, lace or muslin ruched on to a natural wood frame will divide one area from another without making the room oppressive.

Screens need not necessarily be expensive. Old ones can often be bought cheaply in junk shops and, refurbished or re-covered with new fabric and braid, they can take on a new lease of life.

Flight of fantasy
This room is made to look like a conservatory leading on to a grand terrace with a swimming pool. It's just an illusion! Black and white garden furniture set on a tiled floor, plus fretted wooden frieze and plants give a conservatory feel. The terrace view is through a trompe l'oeil window and the slatted screen is painted to resemble folding doors revealing a Mediterranean sky and a swimming pool.

BRIGHT IDEA

SPONGED SCREEN
Make up a screen from lengths of 38mm × 38mm softwood and hardboard. Prime, undercoat and paint the screen with oil-based eggshell paint in off-white. Mark a continuous diagonal line with pencil across the three panels.

Sponge the area above the line on each panel in one colour and the area below in a contrasting or harmonizing one. When completely dry, paint in a solid line, using your pencil marks as a guide, in one of the colours.

◁ **See-through screen**
This lace-covered screen suits the light and airy mood of this neutral room. The style of the screen matches that of the curtains – lightweight fabric hung from a natural wood pole. The screen fabric has a casing along each short end and is then ruched on to the top and bottom rods.

A see-through screen is a good choice for a relatively small room as it separates one area from another without making an oppressive barrier by cutting off the view.

△ **Fabric story**
A simply-shaped bamboo and fabric screen defines a small eating area in a much larger space. The same cream fabric with a woven grid design is used on the screen and to cover the table and chairs. The same type of decorative ties appear on the screen and the 'tea-cosy' chair covers.

▷ **Oriental influence**
Here the screen gives greater importance to traditional furnishings. The nest of mahogany tables and the chair fabric continue the oriental theme; the frames of the tables are turned to resemble bamboo and the design of the chair fabric is of eastern origin.

INDEX

PHOTOGRAPHIC CREDITS
1 Today Interiors, 2-3 Dulux Paints, 4-5 Journal de La Maison, 6 Coloroll, 7 Next Interior, 8(tr) National Magazine Company/David Brittain, 8(tl) National Magazine Company/Hugh Palmer, 8(b) Camera Press, 9 Maison Marie Claire/Scotto/Belmont, 10 National Magazine Company/David Brittain, 11(t) Syndication International, 11(b) National Magazine Company/David Brittain, 12(t) Jalag, 12(b) EWA/Michael Dunne, 13 PWA Internatonal, 14(tl) PWA International, 14(tr) Eximious, 14(b) Arcaid/Annet Held, 15 Derek Middleton, 16(t) EWA/Michael Dunne, 16(b) Derek Middleton, 17(l) Syndication International/Freda Parker, 17(r) Crown Paints, 18(l) EWA/Michael Crockett, 18(r) EWA/Michael Nicholson, 19(t) Crown Paints, 19(b) EWA, 20(t) Jean-Paul Bonhommet, 20(b) Richard Paul, 21 Maison Marie Claire/Hussenot/Penon, 22(t) Camera Press, 22(m) Syndication International, 22(b) National Magazine Company/John Cook, 23(t) Maison Marie Claire/Patau/Bayle, 23(b) National Magazine Company/Jan Baldwin, 24(t) EWA/Spike Powell, 24(b) Jalag/Berndt/Moller, 25(l) Syndication International, 25(r) SaraTaylor/Eaglemoss, 26(t) Dulux Paints, 26(m) Maison Marie Claire/Pataut/Postic, 26(bl) Insight/Linda Burgess, 26(br) Sara Taylor/Eaglemoss, 27 Jean-Paul Bonhommet, 28(t) Next Interior, 28(b) Cover Plus from Woolworth, 29 National Magazine Company/Jan Baldwin, 30(t) EWA/Michael Crockett, 30(b) Maison Marie Claire/Primois/Belmont, 31(t) PWA International, 31(b) Freda Parker/Eaglemoss, 32(t) National Magazine Company/Jan Baldwin, 32(b) Syndication International, 33(l) EWA/Neil Lorimer, 33(r) Crown Paints, 34(t) EWA/Spike Powell, 34(bl) Mr Tomkinsons Carpets, 34(br) EWA/Tom Leighton, 35(t) EWA/Tom Leighton, 35(b) Victor Watts/Over 21, 36(t) Smallbone of Devizes, 36(b) EWA/Clive Helm, 37 Maison Marie Claire/Pataut/Bayle, 38(t) EWA/Michael Dunne, 38(bl) EWA/David Cripps, 38(br) The Picture Library, 39 PWA International, 40(t) EWA/Spike Powell, 40(m) Freda Parker/Eaglemoss 40(b) Jalag/Uhlrich Ruhde, 41(t) Benn Publications, 41(b) Jalag/Uhlrich Ruhde, 42(t) Jalag/Uhlrich Ruhde, 42(b) Benn Publications, 43(t) Maison Marie Claire/Chabaneix/Pench, 43(b) Crown Paints, 44(t & bl) Richard Paul, 44(br) National Magazine Company/John Cook, 45(t) Marks and Spencer plc, 45(b) PWA International, 46 Camera Press, 47(t) PWA International, 47(b) EWA/Michael Crockett, 48(t) Marks and Spencer plc, 48(bl) Coloroll, 48(br) PWA International, 49 EWA/Tom Leighton, 50(t) EWA/Michael Dunne, 50(m) Dulux,

50(b) Jean-Paul Bonhommet, 51 Arthur Sanderson and Sons, 52(t) National Magazine Company/David Brittain, 52(b) EWA/Michael Dunne, 53 EWA/Michael Nicholson, 54(t) Textra, 54(b) PWA International, 55(t) Faber Blinds, 55(b) EWA/Michael Nicholson, 56 EWA/Michael Dunne, 57(t) Interior Selection, 57(b) Antiference, 58(t) Sunway Blinds, 58(bl) Crown Paints, 58(br) EWA/Tim Street-Porter, 59 ICI Fibres, 60(t) Jalag/Peter Adams, 60(bl) EWA/Michael Dunne, 60(br) Arthur Sanderson and Sons, 61 David Hicks/John Spragg, 62(t) David Hicks, 62(bl) Freda Parker/Eaglemoss, 62(br) Jean-Paul Bonhommet, 62(t) The Original Kitchen Company, 63(b) Bo Appeltoft, 64(tl) Guy Bouchet, 64(tr) Osram GEC, 64(b) Guy Bouchet, 65 EWA/Michael Dunne, 66(tl) Freda Parker/Eaglemoss, 66(tr) Charles Hammond, 66(b) National Magazine Company/John Cook, 67 Faber Blinds, 68(b) PWA International, 68-9 EWA, 69(t) EWA/Tim Street-Porter, 69(b) PWA International, 70(t) Dulux, 70(b) Chris Stephens/Eaglemoss, 71(t) Crown Paints 71(bl) Cover Plus from Woolworth, 72(l) Arcaid/Richard Bryant, 72(r) EWA/Michael Dunne, 72(bl) EWA/Michael Dunne, 73 Coloroll, 74(t) Camera Press, 74(b) Syndication International, 75-6 National Magazine Company/Max Roberts, 77 EWA/Michael Dunne, 78(l) Syndication International, 78(r) EWA/Michael Nicholson, 79(t) Nursery Window, 79(b) EWA/Spike Powell, 80(l) Arthur Sanderson and Sons, 80(r) Perrings, 80(b) Kingfisher Wallcoverings, 81 Crown Paints, 82(t) EWA/David Lloyd, 82(b) House of Mayfair, 83(t) Sinclair Nelson Designs, 83(b) Brian Yates Interiors, 84(t) House of Mayfair, 84(b) EWA/Andreas von Einsiedel, 84(br) Arthur Sanderson and Sons, 85 Maison Marie Claire/Pataut/Bayle, 86 National Magazine Company/David Brittain, 87(t) EWA/Clive Helm, 87(b) Dulux, 88(t) EWA/Michael Dunne, 88(b) Dorma, 89 Richard Paul, 90(tl) Tilemart, 90(tr) EWA/Michael Dunne, 90(b) EWA/Jerry Tubby, 91(t) Tilemart, 91(b) Guy Bouchet, 92(t) EWA/Rodney Hyett, 92 Cristal Tiles, 93(l) Richard Paul, 93(r) Syndication International, 94 PWA International.
Front cover: (tl) Robert Harding Syndication/IPC Magazines/Robin Matthews; (tr) Robert Harding Syndication/IPC Magazines/Chris Drake; (bl) Robert Harding Syndication/IPC Magazines/Flavio Gallozzi; (br) Robert Harding Syndication/IPC Magazines/Lucinda Stone.
(EWA - Elizabeth Whiting and Associates)